BE WORTH

FUNDING

Printed in the United States of America

Name: Ty Boone, Author

Title: Be Worth Funding

Summary: With Ty Boone's guidance, readers can gain a deeper understanding of the intricacies of grant writing, funding management, and organizational sustainability. Her unique perspective, honed by years of hands-on experience, offers a fresh and transformative approach to the world of nonprofit fund development.

Identifiers:

978-1-956292-27-5 (Paperback)

978-1-956292-28-2 (Hardcover)

Subjects: Funding Development | Partnerships | Grant Writing

Book Cover Design © 2023 by SUSU Entertainment LLC

BE WORTH FUNDING

Ty Boone

SUSU Entertainment LLC
P.O. Box 1621
Cypress, Texas 77410

CONTENT

INTRODUCTION

Nonprofit organizations are designed to serve the common good. Most work is deserving of funding. Those who need help the most typically deserve help. However, serving a deserving population does not necessarily indicate that an organization itself is worthy of the desired funding or support.

- Deserving refers to something or someone that is entitled to a reward or recognition for their actions or efforts. It implies that the person or thing has earned or worked for the reward.
- Worthy refers to something or someone deserving of respect or recognition for their actions, qualities, or achievements. It implies that the person or thing has a certain level of value or merit.
- In summary, deserving refers to earning something, while worthy refers to having value or merit.

For example, a nonprofit that is dedicated to providing essential resources and support to underserved communities, specifically focusing on education and job training programs, through partnerships with local businesses and government agencies, they have successfully provided job training and placement services, as well as educational opportunities for individuals who may otherwise not have access to these resources. Their programs have been shown to positively impact the lives of those they serve, with many participants reporting increased income and improved job prospects.

Additionally, their work has helped to strengthen the local economy by providing a skilled workforce for businesses. Overall, this organization is worth funding as they are making a tangible difference in the lives of those they serve and contributing to the betterment of their community.

Funding worthiness also helps an organization understand where they stand and how they compete compared to other organizations. The ability of your organization to compete predicts its ability to consistently attract funding and sustain. Several factors make an organization competitive for funding. They include:

1. Strong and clear mission: Funders want to see that a nonprofit has a well-defined mission that aligns with their own goals and values.

2. Proven track record: Nonprofits with a history of successfully achieving their goals and demonstrating impact are more likely to receive funding.

3. Strategic plan: A well-thought-out strategic plan that outlines the nonprofit's goals, strategies, and action steps can demonstrate to funders that the organization is well-managed and focused on achieving its mission.

4. Strong leadership: Nonprofits with strong and effective leadership are more likely to be successful in achieving their goals and, as a result, more likely to receive funding.

5. Diversified funding: Nonprofits with a diversified funding base, including a mix of government grants, foundation grants, and individual donations, are more likely to be sustainable over the long term.

6. Strong partnerships: Nonprofits that have strong partnerships with other organizations and stakeholders in their community can demonstrate to funders that they are well-connected and able to leverage resources effectively.

7. Clear and measurable goals: Funders want to see that a nonprofit has clear and measurable goals, so they can track its progress and understand the impact of their funding.

A nonprofit's mission allows supporters to understand what an organization does now. How do you make a difference now? A good mission typically answers directly or indirectly the following questions:

1) Who are you?

2) Who do you serve?

3) How do you serve?

4) What difference do you make?

Take a look at this mission statement:

"To strengthen and support underprivileged communities by providing access to education, healthcare, and necessities, fostering self-sufficiency, and promoting social and economic development."

In this example, "to strengthen and support" would equate to the difference being made. "Under-resourced communities" identifies who is being served. "Providing access to education, healthcare, and necessities for fostering self-sufficiency, and promoting social and economic development" tells us how they are served.

Competitive and funding-worthy organizations should also possess a proven track record. A proven nonprofit track record refers to a history of successfully achieving the mission and goals of a nonprofit organization. This can include a history of raising funds, providing services to the community, and achieving measurable impact in the areas they serve.

It also includes a good reputation in the community, positive relationships with stakeholders, and a strong governance and management structure. A nonprofit with a proven track record is considered a reliable and effective organization by donors, funders, and the community. Strategic planning is an area many new and under-experienced organizations fail to address. A nonprofit strategic plan is a document that outlines the organization's mission, goals, and objectives, as well as the strategies and actions that will be taken to achieve them. It serves as a roadmap for the organization's future, outlining the direction it will take to fulfill its mission and achieve its goals.

It also includes metrics to measure progress and evaluate success. The strategic plan is typically reviewed and updated regularly to ensure that the organization is on track to achieve its goals and adapt to any changes in the external environment. Strategic planning and implementation of developed strategies help position organizations for success.

While we like the idea of grant funding, grants are never guaranteed. Despite the success rate of your grant writer, even the best writers lose some. The ability to diversify your funding efforts allows your organization to do the work and gives you the ability to carry out your mission regardless of grant denial.

Nonprofit diversified funding refers to the practice of obtaining funding from multiple sources rather than relying on a single source of funding. This can include a combination of government grants, private donations, corporate sponsorships, and earned income from program services or events. Diversifying funding sources helps nonprofits to mitigate the risk of losing funding from a single source and ensures a more stable financial footing for the organization. Worthy organizations understand why they should not put "all of their eggs in one basket."

Diversity comes in several ways. In addition to diversified funding efforts, funders and supporters like to see that your organization can "work well with others." Additionally, they prefer that they get the biggest bang for their buck when and if they support you. Although there is some tendency in the field to be territorial, nonprofit organizations are usually stronger together. This is why partnerships are important. Partnerships can be represented in ways such as:

1. Collaboration between a nonprofit organization and a government agency to provide services and resources to underserved communities.

2. Partnership between a nonprofit and a for-profit company to increase funding and resources for a specific cause or project.

3. Alliance between multiple nonprofits working together to achieve a shared goal or mission.

4. Joint venture between a nonprofit and a local business to provide job training and employment opportunities for disadvantaged individuals.

5. Partnership between a nonprofit and a school district to provide educational programs and resources for low-income students.

6. Collaboration between a nonprofit and a healthcare organization to provide health services and education to underserved populations.

A. Partnership between a nonprofit and a religious organization to provide volunteer opportunities and community outreach services.

B. Alliance between a nonprofit and a community organization to provide services and resources to immigrants and refugees.

C. Joint venture between a nonprofit and a conservation organization to protect and preserve natural resources and wildlife habitats.

D. Partnership between a nonprofit and a research institution to conduct studies and develop new treatments and therapies for specific diseases or conditions.

More than many other factors, funders want to be able to trust your organization's work and believe that your programs do what you claim. Measurable goals and outcomes provide the evidence funders need to trust your work. Some examples of measurable goals and outcomes might include:

1. Increasing the number of volunteers by 25% within the next six months.

2. Raising $50,000 in funding through a fundraising campaign within the following year.

3. Improving clients' overall satisfaction by 50% within the next two years by implementing new programs and services.

4. Increasing the number of individuals served by the organization by 30% within the next three years.

5. Increasing the number of community partnerships by 50% within the following year.

6. Improving the overall organizational efficiency by 20% within the next year by implementing new technology and process improvements.

7. Increasing the number of social media followers by 50% within the next six months.

8. Increasing the number of donations made by repeat donors by 25% within the following year.

9. Reducing the number of client complaints by 50% within the next six months.

10. Increasing the overall awareness of the organization by 40% within the next year through targeted marketing and outreach efforts.

At this point, we can see that funding worthiness reaches beyond basic nonprofit business formation.

WORTHY LEADERSHIP AND SYSTEMS

Of course, an organization can only be as successful as its leadership. Nonprofit leadership should be visionary and strategic, with a clear understanding of the organization's mission and goals. It should be collaborative, involving all stakeholders in decision-making and ensuring that all voices are heard. It should be transparent and accountable, with clear communication and reporting on the organization's activities and outcomes.

Nonprofit leaders should also be ethical and responsible, with a commitment to social justice and community impact. They should be adaptable and responsive to changing circumstances and be able to navigate through challenges and crises. Overall, nonprofit leaders should be focused on creating positive change and making a meaningful impact in the community.

Leadership is your board of directors. Leadership is your executive staff. Your Executive Director, and your CEO, are all considered leaders. Often, when an organization fails to function properly, the issue lies with those in leadership. Typically, the issue is that leaders do not fully understand the organization's mission, have not bought into the organization's mission, and/or do not know how to create an environment that facilitates the strategic implementation of fund development and program growth.

You want people on your board who are committed. You want people who have connections with the community. You want people who are contributing. Sometimes we forget about that when we are eager to get started. Most states require at least three board members in order to recognize your organization as a nonprofit. Board members are a required foundational component for nonprofit organizations. However, do not let this pressure you into bringing the wrong people on board.

You want to have board members who are competent. They don't have to have a Ph.D. to be on a nonprofit board or a degree in micro-physics, but you want to have someone who cares, not only about the population that your organization will serve but competent and committed to the vision of the nonprofit and the community.

Most of the time, that's where we fall short. We get people who are committed to us, by agreeing to be on the board, however, when it's time to work in the organization, they can't do it because they're not committed to the cause and the vision in the same manner that you are. They're not committed in a way that will assist you in moving your organization forward. Then, you have your bosses, of course. You know, those people who are in director positions, such as: CEOs, Presidents, Vice-Presidents, and Executive Directors. Next, is the central administration. Central administration would be those people who would make sure the wheels are turning. They are your program guides and resource providers. These are the people who are mostly involved with the implementation of the mission.

If you get people on the board who are your friends, they may potentially find it difficult to separate friendship roles and behaviors from the roles, duties and responsibilities of a board member. As the saying goes, "Never mix business with pleasure." Your friends will agree to serving as a board member because they don't want to say no to you. They don't want to let you down. So, they'll get on your board, and then you'll find out when it's time to put your feet on the pavement, your friends may say things like, "Look, I'm tired, I've got something else to do," and not take their board duties and responsibilities seriously.

It is ultimately best to avoid placing family members on the board of a nonprofit public charity. However, the Internal Revenue Service (IRS) does currently consider an organization within ethical bounds if the board is made up of no more than 49% of individuals who are related. Nevertheless, having family members on board can result in conflict and major tension. Funders can also view this negatively as they conclude that because of family relationships, accountability, particularly fiscal accountability may be low.

As to be expected, the success and sustainability of an organization starts with the effectiveness of its leadership. Often, when you're leading with passion, and you have love in your heart for the community, that's when you decide that you're ready to be a founder of an organization.

However, the first thing you must keep in mind is that just because you are the founder does not necessarily mean that you must be the person who is leading everything; you don't have to be the Executive Director or CEO. In fact, many founders stay in the lane of "visionary," while others are hired to lead the organization.

While you do not have to be a rocket scientist to lead an organization, you will certainly need to engage in nonprofit education and continuing education in leadership and management to ensure your organization's success. Get educated in the business of nonprofits. Larger, better funded organizations usually hire staff to serve in leadership positions.

These positions come with qualification requirements that include education, experience, or a combination of both. To compete for funding at the same level that these organizations compete, you must be willing to expand your knowledge as it relates to the business (organization) that you are leading. Consistently supported and funded organizations have strong leaders, who know the business of nonprofits, and who continue to be educated in the business of nonprofits.

Think about it. If you're a nonprofit Executive Director or nonprofit CEO, and I come to you and ask, "May I write you this grant for $500,000?" You in return pay me $10,000 to write this grant, but you are not familiar with grant writing; you're not familiar with the business of nonprofits; you don't know if you are competitive for this particular funding opportunity or not.

You don't know the basic business of nonprofits because you think that a grant writer will solve your money problems. You are likely to take a chance and pay the grant writing fee (regardless of how you find the funds) because you assume that the investment is worth the risk. However, although grants are never guaranteed, the more you know about your own level of readiness, the more informed decisions you can make in situations like this.

Your board and executive staff are especially important because they must help facilitate your mission and assist with progressing you toward your vision. Do you have board support? If your board is not supporting you, do not expect others to support you. Does your organization have a relationship with the community? Do you have a credible track record? In addition to your organization's track record, do you know the track records, credibility, and integrity of those in charge of representing your organization?

When you're doing things like fundraising, for example, many states require that you register to fundraise. Those states also conduct background checks on the person or persons who are going to oversee handling the money. Have you been arrested for money fraud? Do you have a criminal record? Do you know how to manage finances? Are you credible in the areas of finance and fiscal responsibility?

To consistently attract outside support, an organization must function well internally. It is ultimately the job of the executive staff to ensure that the internal functions are conducive to support. "Many organizations, particularly those founded and led by the same individual, are likely to struggle in this area." As the Executive Director (or CEO as many are titled, regardless of size), it is your job to track the success of the organization and to be able to identify shortcomings. Likewise, conversations regarding this are to be had with your board. The board is not only supposed to be aware of your funding goals but should help you to create them and meet them. Unfortunately, many under-experienced or under-educated boards, particularly of new and developing organizations, do very little to elevate the organization.

Many do this not because they do not wish to be good leaders but because they have not been adequately informed of their roles within the organizations and are not held accountable in the roles they agreed to occupy. Ultimately, this leaves the organization in the position to not attract funds or to attract them so inconsistently that it fails fast.

The effort and effectiveness of the team (which includes paid as well as volunteer staff) are set in motion by the effort and effectiveness of leadership. For the most part, the team is made up of individuals who are important in executing and mobilizing the day-to-day operations and programs. These people are highly important because they usually get their hands dirty, boots on the ground, and create impact. With this, it is important to remember that an organization is not a one-man show. Although we easily find ourselves going at it alone when not built properly, an organization, by definition, is a group of individuals working toward a common goal. If you do not have people working with you, whether one person or 50 people, you technically do not have an organization.

An organization involves a group of people. Whether you are ready to hire staff, or your staff is volunteering, this remains the same. Having a team helps to position your organization for funding. How? A team can implement your programs and services and you can show proof of work.

Along with leadership, another area where organizations fall short is their systems. While leading with passion is a desired quality, having the proper systems in place will ensure that your organization runs smoothly and that your infrastructure can manage the tasks associated with development growth and sustainability.

As it pertains to systems, every organization needs to have, at minimum, the following systems or system concepts in place:

A System For Managing Donations:

There are tons of donor management software/CRM available. Without getting into favoring one above the other, donor management allows you to streamline and organize the donation process. As your organization grows, something that sounds as painless as accepting and processing donations can quickly become overwhelming if not managed correctly.

A System For Paying the Bills and Managing Expenses:

This refers to the process used to receive and spend money. Knowing who signs the checks and why.

A System for Managing Bank Accounts, Filing, Record-keeping, and Fiscal Accountability:

This is in connection with oversight that is given above and beyond basic oversight. Who is holding whom accountable? What are your bookkeeping responsibilities and practices?

"Do you have accounting systems in place? One of the major concerns that I see in underfunded nonprofits, especially those who have very small budgets, is the lack of audited financials. Not having audited financials when the funder is requiring one is a good indication that you are not ready for the grant or level of grant that you are seeking.

While some may encourage work-a-rounds to this, I sincerely believe that organizations are more competitive when they have what the funder requires. Additionally, the inability to obtain things like audited financials that funders hold as important, gives funders the impression that the organization is not functioning properly and that it does not know how to attract funding for what they need. When this is the perspective, it is harder for the funder to trust you to serve effectively, manage funds and reach the impact they'd like to see accomplished with their funding.

A System for Protecting Data and Managing Risk:

Many organizations are privy to client data and information. How is that information protected? What processes are put in place to address crisis or risk? How are problems solved? Who is responsible for process improvement?

A System for Communication:

This establishes the proper communication protocol (whether spoken, written, or otherwise) both inside and outside of the organization. While technology has truly become a leading way to gain support, many are continuing to use the traditional mail approach. If those who support you aren't particularly "tech savvy" people, you will need to appeal to them by using their most desired platform. Do you have a communication feature, a way to say thank you for your contributions?

A System for Program and Service Establishment, Implementation, and Graduation:

This includes processes such as, onboarding clients or program participants, determining their program and/or service fit, establishing and executing the program or service model, and ultimately through evaluation, addressing benchmarks and milestones necessary to have participants terminate or graduate from services. What are the details of your program, and what problems does it solve? How are you prioritizing the needs of your program? If your organization has multiple programs, which program is priority for funding? Based on your organization's capacity, is which program are you best equipped to grow first?

As someone who has worked with a variety of organizations of different sizes, it has been observed more often than not that while all organizations are different, there is one commonality: the need and desire for funding or more funding.

New and under-experienced organizations are sometimes misled to think that funding comes before the work. However, this could not be further from the truth. Funders, grant makers, sponsors, and donors like to see that your organization is putting forth the work before handing over their money to you.

Organizations that do not understand that serving comes before funding usually find themselves rejected for funding opportunities because there is no real proof of impact. Additionally, we can gain the trust of funders when they see that we are putting in the work. Putting in the work allows you to present your organization in a more funding-worthy light.

One of my favorite mantras is, "Get Visible. Get Moving. Get Funded." These three steps will get you close to positioning and sustaining your organization because we live in a society where people want things fast, and the willingness and patience to properly position flies out of the window when we are seeking funding.

A problem that usually plagues smaller organizations is that while the heart to serve is huge, the money to serve typically comes in inconsistently or not at all. Much of this is the result of poor positioning early on. Most of the time, many organizations are led by someone with a heart to serve. This is especially true if the organization is ultimately being led by the founder. Unfortunately, many of these organizations fail and fail quickly because passion does not necessarily pay if the organization itself is not in a position for funding.

Positioning is a process, and the best place to start is with an organizational self-reflection and self-assessment of where your organization stands regarding positioning for success and sustainability. Some lingering questions for underfunded organizations include, ""Why are other organizations getting all the money?" Why are we not seeing funding success?" "Why is my organization struggling while those around me seem to flourish?"

I often see celebrations on social media when an organization has received nonprofit/501c3 approval. Although it is awesome achievement, forgive me if I do not celebrate. My lack of enthusiasm is the result of the fact that 501c3 approval does not equal funding. What does approval mean if you are unable to attract the support that you need to build and grow a successful organization? Without proper positioning, your IRS approval letter (Determination Letter) is just a piece of paper. You want to make sure that you make this paperwork for you.

Because most underfunded organizations are looking for "right now" funding, it is difficult to think about the future and sustainability. However, funders want to know your plans to sustain. It makes perfect sense for a grant funder to ask you about your sustainability plan. Primarily because they want to know that your organization will yield a good return on their investment. They want to be assured that once their funding is spent, your organization will continue to grow, and your programs will continue to produce results. They do not want to fund your organization today only to see that it has failed a year later.

Are you paying attention to service trends and funding trends? Trends can certainly affect your ability to sustain.

Did you know that just because somebody needed something five years ago, it doesn't necessarily mean they need that thing now? Changes in your community's needs can affect how you serve. Are you aware of the changes? Are your policies clear? Do you have operation procedures in place? Do you have ways to manage your donors? Do you have databases for your programs? Do you know how to accept gifts? Do you have a donate button on your website? Do you have a call to action on your website? Do you have a fundraising strategy in place, or are you just popping up? Are you going around with a white envelope, randomly asking for money? It is your duty to know those from whom you are seeking support. How do they like to give?

WORTHY PARTNERSHIPS

Do you have a network of potential partners? Think about that just for a minute and decide. Consider making a list of potential partners and small businesses in your community. You don't have to minimize them to only nonprofit organizations, they can be just people in the community. They can also be small for-profit businesses, but who can you reach out to be a part of your network?

Partnerships are a great way to bring credibility to your organization. Partnerships are key in accomplishing large goals and could be the exact piece of the puzzle that is needed to ensure that you manifest your vision. Prior to initiating a partnership with another entity or organization, you want to make sure that you are sufficient enough to offer something that the partner would be willing to accept. You also want to make sure that your prospective partner has good partnership qualities.

Think of it like a relationship that leads to marriage. When you are entering or considering entering the serious stage of the relationship, you take a personal assessment: What do I have to offer? What do they have to offer? If nobody has anything to offer, then together, we have nothing. This, of course, is not a great way to enter into a marriage, just as it is not a good way to enter into a working relationship or partnership.

However, if your partner has something and you have that same something, this simply means that you have more of that something. More is better, right? If one of you are lacking in one space but has enough to cover in a different space, then the partner fills the space where there is a lack, but together you are complete. This same scenario applies when you are seeking to partner with your organization. How can that thing you have, increase that thing they have? Or how can that thing that they don't have be magnified by the thing that you do have?

"Most new and under-developed organizations go the wrong way into partnerships. They ask, "What's in it for me?" When the focus, in fact, should be, "What do I bring to the table? ... and how can what I bring to the table ensure that we all eat a well-balanced and healthy meal?" You want your partner to feel that you bring something that will help them to get to the next level of growth.

Although the next level of growth is the ultimate outcome, going into the partnership, you will want to look more at your mission than at your vision. Your mission is what you are doing now. Your vision is what you plan to do at some point in the future. Going back to the relationship and marriage scenario, what you are doing now provides proof that you can achieve your goals in the future.

You want your potential partner to see you as, "partnership potential." If you are unable to prove that you are stable now, it will be difficult to trust that you can succeed in the future. Therefore, when seeking partnership, evidence of what you have accomplished already, and what you are currently accomplishing, gives you more "brownie points" than what you plan to do in the future, particularly, if your future goals are too lofty to comprehend for those whom you do not yet have a relationship with. Once your partner can see that you are making momentum within your mission, they are going to be more willing to help you to achieve your vision.

Think about businesses, organizations, or other entities in your community that you would like to partner with. Make a list of them and summarize why they would be a good partner and how partnering with your organization helps them to achieve their next level. Their next-level goals could be related to visibility, service, operations, funding, sustainability, or some unique mixture of those five areas. Then think of how they can also support you while you walk out of your current mission and achieve your most immediate goals.

Your partner(s) do not necessarily have to be other nonprofit businesses. For example, if you are working with youth, potential partners might be a private pediatric dentist's office downtown, a potential partner might be the school, or a potential partner might be the daycare on the other side of town. Your priority populations are the same or similar. You are seeking to serve a similar audience. With this, you do not have to convince them that there is a need for youth-focused services in your area. They are already in the area. They serve whom you serve. They understand the need.

Your partner could be operating in the same or different space as your organization. For example, if you are a youth service organization, it is perfectly fine to partner with another youth service organization. It is also acceptable that the organizations have the same or similar programs. However, it is important to understand that where the same or similar programs exist, it is the obligation of each involved partner to identify and fill the gaps of the other partner or to purposefully strengthen identified areas where you would be stronger together.

Suppose that your organization helps students improve their ACT test scores for college entry. The organization across town also offers ACT prep. However, while their organization offers general remediation, your organization has trained math specialists who can work with students; recognizing that math is a troublesome testing area. Proposing to provide math support to the organization across town would allow you both to meet your goals of increasing ACT scores, increasing college acceptance rates, and improving the math scores of those you serve. Joining forces makes it possible to serve bigger and fosters opportunities to attract funding more consistently together.

Partnering successfully also suggests that your organization understands the role of partnerships in sustainability and impact.

Partnering allows you to reach more members of your priority population through your work. Take, for example, that alone you have the capacity to serve 50 people. When trying to communicate your service numbers, 50 may appear low depending on the type of funding you are seeking, and the level of funding awarded.

Let's assume that your partner's organization serves 400 people. Together you serve 450 people. This looks better than 50, especially when you are seeking substantial funding from certain caliber grants, etc. Unfortunately, knowing whom they serve is not by itself a reason to initiate a partnership.

Never forget to research your potential partner before reaching out for a partnership. Find out what it is that they do, what they are doing, how they are doing it, and what success they have had with it. Then, determine how what you do can add to their success.

For example, if the pediatric dental office is offering dental hygiene products to high school students, and your organization helps high school students increase their ACT scores, wouldn't it be great if the dental office provided hygiene products to your students? Would distributing their products to your students increase the number of clients they have?

This would be particularly rewarding if they are seeking new clients. In your research, have you discovered that children with healthier hygiene habits are more likely to test well? Could the dental office refer students to your organization for your programs and services when searching for and seeking partnership opportunities? Your organization should be aware of how it makes a great partner. As a potential partner your organization should have remarkable proof of what it does and what it can do to help the prospective partner(s) reach its goals.

For example, if you say that you provide math remediation and there is no one on your staff, team, or volunteers that is skilled at math, it is going to be hard to convince a partner, supporter, or funder that you can do what you say you can do. You cannot accurately communicate to the potential partner, funder, or sponsor that you know how to successfully do what it is that you say you do. However, if your team, staff, and/or volunteers represent the desired experience and data shows relevant success, potential supporters will see your credibility and are more willing to support you.

Why community partnerships? When positioned correctly, communities find nonprofit organizations beneficial. Communities are a great source of networking, partnerships, and funding. The great thing about community funds is that you're going to be able to touch several lives across the community, and that's why community grants are so important. "Many times, organizations are denied community level funding because our requests are too self-focused or focused on only our individual organization."

What funders want us to do is inform them how our receiving their support will benefit the community (or population) we serve as a whole. When showing your ability to work well with others, you communicate that you understand the importance of partnerships. You know how relationships increase capacity and sustainability. Funders want to see that you're going to be able to exist for a long time, and when you have created good relationships with the community, that's it, right? That's your bridge to the next thing.

For those services that you can't provide, developing partnerships to fill those gaps helps to guide your organization to the next level, while ensuring its ability to sustain itself. On the other hand, if you're providing a service, or if you want to provide a service that you're not quite ready to provide, let's say for example, you're doing case management, and you'd like housing to be a part of what you do, but you don't provide housing, you provide counseling, if there is a community organization in your community that does provide housing, being able to connect with them shows the fact that you know how to work well with others.

You know how to make this happen. You know how to reach the goal of providing housing, even if they were put here just to provide counseling services, especially if the funder's goal is to provide housing. You want to make sure that what you're doing is important enough that other people in the community understand the importance and that you find community groups and community organizations that can help you fill in the gaps. Ultimately, having partners can increase your ability to attract new funds and retain old ones.

Take, for example, something on a larger scale, such as a federal grant. Federal grants are often huge and offer multiple funding years. Let's pretend that there is a $3 million dollar funding opportunity available, because funding this large value impacts everything. They understand that the best way to facilitate impact is to be able to reach or serve outside of the confines of a single organization.

This is why these types of applications ask questions such as, "Who are your business partners?" If you've ever gotten into a federal grant opportunity or even a large foundation grant, you are no stranger to this line of questioning. "Who do you work with within the community? Who are your community partners?"

Many of us talk ourselves out of funding opportunities because we want to stay inside of the box. We're territorial. We don't want to work with other people. The failure or inability to develop and sustain partnerships and relationships is the leading reason why nonprofit organizations fail.

Get out and network for the purpose of building community relationships so that you can get more funding for your organization.

Even if you're just saying, "Hey, we'll send people there, but we're not giving them any money." "Collaborating and partnering shows the funder to see that you're working with others, and you know how to share responsibility and how to meet goals."

Lots of new and under-experienced organizations are run by lone leaders. I use the term "lone leaders" to refer to the fact that many founders turn into Executive Directors or CEOs and are thrown into running and leading the organizations by themselves. Although an organization, by definition, is a "group" of people working together to reach coming business goals, this sometimes does not happen right away for most grassroots and traditionally started community-based organizations.

Starting alone usually means that the organization does not have the fiscal strength to do work to the level desired. They typically do not have the capacity to perform at levels that will attract funding consistently. However, this looks different if the organizations know how to attract and leverage partnerships. When organizations work together, the funder gets to see how this work leads to a greater impact. Greater demonstration of impact leads to better funding opportunities.

Partnerships and approaching them should not be taken lightly. Before you seek partners, you must first know a few things about your own organization. The first thing that you will need to know is who you are. The answer to who you are starts with what your mission is. What is that thing or those things that you do daily? What is the problem you solve? How do you solve that problem or problems?

This is to be understood before seeking to join forces with others; because if you are not clear on what you do, why, and how you do it, it will be more difficult to know where or how you fit as a partner. Potential partners also must know what you bring to the table. What do you have to offer? What are the goals of this partnership? How do you plan to meet these goals? How will entering a partnership help you to reach these goals more effectively and efficiently?

For example, if you're going out and you're seeking someone to provide housing for those you serve, you will know answers to questions for your organization such as: How many people do we serve? How many units of housing do we need? How many units do we currently have? How can this partnership help us to improve the service we provide?

How can the service we provide, or a different relevant service benefit the potential partner? When you are prepared with answers to questions such as these, you allow the potential partner to see more clearly how the partnership is mutually beneficial. They understand how they can help you to make your situation better. However, they can also imagine how working with you will help move them closer to their goals as well.

On the other hand, if you are seeking partnerships and you do not yet understand your role in the potential relationship, potential partners see you as "scrambling." They do not feel that you are clear about what you do, how you serve, and how what you do affects them. When this happens, especially with potential partners with whom you have not already developed a rapport, they are more likely to respond negatively to your desire to work together or partner. If you do not clearly understand how you bring value to the potential partnership, you are also not likely to understand what value your potential partner will bring to you.

To further establish the partnership, make sure that you have a Memorandum of Understanding (MOU or sometimes called MOA for Memorandum of Agreement) in place. An MOU defines what you will bring to the table, what your partner(s) brings to the table, and what you should expect from the deal. You want to know what's in it for you, and you want to be able to tell them what's in it for them.

Not every opportunity to collaborate is one you should become involved with. While collaborations carry a shorter, less strict commitment than partnerships, mismatched collaborations could also produce poor funding-worthy results for your organization. Take, for example, the infamous "back-to-school drives" and "backpack rallies."

Before agreeing to participate, you first want to know whether your participation helps you to continue to serve your priority population. What do you benefit from participating in the event? Are you able to capture data, and if so, how is that data relevant to your organization's mission? Of course, if you are seeking community visibility or utilizing the event as an opportunity to identify those in possible need of your service, participation is not necessarily a bad thing.

Let's say that your organization's mission has a healthcare focus, and you need support from sponsors who have a special interest in healthcare. While pharmaceutical companies often get a bad rap, they are a great sponsorship source, particularly for needs related to healthcare and health education.

What kind of gaps can you fill? Stop being territorial!

Your mission should be a direct reflection of what you do. If your mission says that we are serving marginalized low-income individuals, middle-income people should not be in the social impact part of your organization. Too often, small, under-experienced organizations lose valuable resources because they want to help everyone. Helping others is good. We are in the social impact business, public charity, and "heart work," to do just that. However, organizations must be certain that their resources are properly guided. This is not to say that you cannot extend your services if the extension further supports your mission. Nevertheless, your core services should be directed at the intended segment of the population you were formed to serve.

WORTHY SPONSORSHIP

There are several ways to generate funding for your organization. Sponsorship is on my list of favorites. When done correctly, sponsorships are an amazing way to generate support. When done incorrectly, seeking sponsorships can result in a lot of lost time and effort and ends in frustration.

The most common mistake that people make when seeking sponsorships is not setting a sensible sponsorship goal. The goal involves several factors including: How much money are you trying to attract through sponsorships? Why were this amount chosen? What will you do with the money? And most importantly, who are you going to ask?

How much to ask for depends on your realistic sponsorship goals. The reality of goals takes shape once the organization understands its mission, understands those who support its cause, can identify supporters, can communicate impact, has become visible, and built relationships either directly or indirectly with potential sponsors.

Understanding what the money will help you to accomplish and the costs associated with that will help you to form the dollar amount of your goal.

One of the most important aspects of sponsorships is finding the right sponsor. How many times have you spent countless hours drafting mailing sponsorship packets, letters, and emails only to get a sucky response? Approaching the right sponsor requires research to first determine whether a sponsor is a good fit.

Research also helps you to establish ideas for how much they give. In addition to this, it is always important to get your board involved. Your board should be connected to the degree that they are able to point you in the direction of potential sponsors and supporters. With your board, you can create a solid "hit list" (list of potential sponsors to target for your sponsorship goals).

When I think of "hit list," I imagine the duties of an assassin. You are the assassin. Whom are you targeting? Whom will you hit? Honestly, I have never been an assassin. I just watch them on television. Nevertheless, think about it. Assassin movies. The assassin will get this list that tells them whom they want and whom the person who hired them wants them to go after.

The individuals on the hit list will have certain characteristics. They will fit a specific profile. In this same instance, you determine your sponsorship goal, and you are ready to create a hit list of people, sponsors, etc., who can help you to reach that goal.

Pretend that you have a fundraising goal of $5,000.00, which is a small amount, however, you will need to know who you will ask. Do you have a donor list already? If you do not, you must create one. This is where your board comes in handy. Have them to assist you in identifying people, corporations, and other businesses most likely to support your cause. Start with their recommendations. Considering a simple $5,000 goal. With a goal this small, you would not need a bunch of millionaires to help you reach this goal. However, you will need enough people to give the right amount of money if you plan to reach your goal.

How many people do you have on your hit list, and what kind of givers are they? If your hit list is filled with people who are not likely to give more than $5, you will need a larger hit list. However, if your list contains those who give a lot more, how many of those people do you have?

One reason we are missing the mark and ending up with unsuccessful fundraisers is that our funding raising goals and our target audience (those whom we want to support us) do not match. For example, lots of nonprofits seek out celebrity sponsorship either before they are ready, before they have demonstrated impact, or before they understand their fundraising goals. Typically, celebrities give big when they care big. With this, asking celebrities for $10 to help you reach your funding goal seems suspicious.

Particularly, if the organization is not already highly visible and does not already have evident solid support. Asking for $10 from someone who is accustomed to giving thousands (or more) communicates that you either have tons of people giving you $10, so your goal is within reach, or that you do not know enough about the giving pattern of your target audience to ask for the right amount of support.

Most organizations can secure $5,000 in support with very little effort. Sponsorship requests such as those you see with banks and small businesses, micro-grants that do not require a high skill level of grant writing, etc., can all help achieve this goal if approached strategically.

While sponsorship letters and sponsorship decks serve their purpose, they are usually more of a miss than a hit for lots of organizations. This is because we spend a lot of money on the graphic design of the deck, publishing, printing, and ensuring that they are "pretty." However, we do not spend enough time selling the organization and communicating how supporting the organization truly makes a measurable and worthwhile difference.

Not that direct mail has completely died or going anywhere soon (despite technology), but we are continuing to mail out letters in the absence of establishing a direct or indirect relationship with would-be sponsors. As a result, our sponsorship letters and decks are likely to remain ignored or simply thrown away with the morning's trash.

Ultimately, when you are asking for other people's money, particularly on the level of sponsorships, they want to know the answers to questions such as: 1) "Why have you chosen to ask me for money?" 2) "Why should I give my money to your organization?" 3) "How much money do you want?" 4) "How does my giving to your organization benefit me and my business?"

Sponsorship letters carry various formats. However, a great story is always a good way to get people to commit to reading your letter. One turn-off I see in many letters is including, "We are a 501c3," in the introductory sentence or paragraph. Normally, if you are reaching out for a sponsorship or a donation for your "organization," it is assumed that you are a 501c3. If you need to clarify, do so. However, since it is already understood, including it in the opening, especially if you include it ahead of your impact story or transformational content, can disengage the reader too early.

Use the opening to draw in your audience. Tell me what a day in the life of your organization looks like. Share your wins and perspectives of those you serve. Discuss how the service you provide has made a difference and give examples where you can. More important than how you present your introduction is your relationships. In the world of "funding worthiness," relationships truly do matter. All things aside, you can submit a poorly written sponsorship request or even grant application in some cases, and if you have built a relationship with the sponsor or funder, you could get away with it. This is yet another reason why electing strong board members for your organization is very important. As connected leaders in the community representing your organization, they can be the bridge between your organization and potential donors and sponsors.

WORTHY PROGRAMS

Organizations grow best when people, processes, and programs are in place. Unfortunately, organizations that do not grow to become sustainable are typically those with poorly developed people, processes, or programs.

The inability to develop properly often leaves organizations with limited capacity and leadership. Additionally, when the organization is not properly developed, it quickly falls into the loop of delivering activities and events in the name of being "visible" or giving back and not fully established programs.

Programs solve problems. Funders pay to have problems solved. If your organization understands program development and can successfully implement programs and communicate impact, funding is easier to obtain and can be obtained more consistently.

Programs are what you need to get your organization to the next level. A lot of people think that they have programs when they're in fact simply hosting events, or implementing a bunch of activities, not producing a real outcome, not producing any solid, measurable results. They're finding themselves struggling year after year, in the same activities and not being able to attract funding.

For example, every summer you have the popular backpack and back-to-school rallies that take place every summer, asking individuals to give your organization money for backpacks and supplies for the community. Every year, it seems to be a struggle to get the same people to give money for the back-to-school drive.

The back-to-school rallies is not a program, it is an activity. It is something that you are doing, possibly to bring more visibility to your organization, but the back-to-school rally by itself does not solve a problem. While it addresses a temporary concern, the deeper underlying problem, which is perhaps, poor economic health in communities, poor literacy skills, and school retention that is not solved, addressed, or approached. While people come out to the back-to-school rallies and we can report their attendance, we cannot use the event alone to confirm that the rallies increased literacy rates, changed economic health, or made school retention rates better.

So often, people who are showing up for these events simply to show that they came out. However, if you can't make a difference in the lives of those people who got a backpack, you did not produce an outcome and funds or fund outcomes. They want to see that you've made an impact. They want to see that you have produced a change in these people that you were serving.

If not, their investment does not have a good return. They don't care about giving backpacks to people if the backpack is not going to make a difference. What is it about this backpack? What is the service that you're providing along with this backpack? What's going to create a difference in the lives of people that you're giving the backpacks to?

Before you can consistently attract funding, programs are to be in place. You want to make sure that you have programs and that your programs are built solid. You want to make sure that you're producing outcomes, and that you're creating an impact that the funder wants to support. This applies whether you are seeking grant funding, sponsorship support, or other support. The sponsor wants to know that if money is given, it is going to have a lasting effect. Whether the gift is $20 or $200,000, the funder wants to know that the award was not given in vain. Sadly, this is where we often miss the mark.

Take, for example, that you need to have fifty backpacks sponsored for your back-to-school rally. The sponsor gives you $1,000 but does not hear from you again until the next year at your back-to-school rally, and you're asking them for $1,000 again. This time before they give, they're trying to find out what in the world happened with this $1,000 they gave you last year. The only thing you can say to them is that you delivered backpacks. What you cannot answer is what happened after the backpacks were received.

Did the backpacks include information that helped parents change their economic situations so that they can purchase backpacks for their children next year on their own? Did the backpacks serve as an invite to ACT prep or math remediation so that the students could become better prepared for college? Or was there some form of follow-up to determine whether the students carried the backpacks to school? If yes, was there a difference in behavior, a difference in grades for those who carried your backpacks based on what your goals were?

As it relates to programs, a program transforms the event into a system that solves a problem. For example, we are focusing on increasing ACT scores. While we host the back-to-school drive, the backpack is filled with ACT prep information, an invitation to our ACT prep program, math and science study tips, and college admissions information.

If you are going to improve ACT scores, and this encompasses your mission, how do you need to accomplish this? Start with the backpack rally as the starting point of visibility and recruitment for your program? What do you need? You need staff. You need ACT prep guides. You possibly need laptops. You need bookbags, etc. These things are considered inputs. These things will also help you to determine how much money you need for your program. If you don't know what you need, you don't know what you're paying for. If you don't know what you're paying for, you don't know what to ask the sponsor for. You don't know what to ask the funder for.

So often, we go in blindly with no programs in place, and we try to work backward based on the funding opportunity, especially when there is a grant announcement. Before you ask a sponsor for a dime, before you apply for grants, you should know what you need. You should have your program and your model together before submitting a funding announcement. It is not the time to create your program; you should be doing it now so that you're going to be ready to apply this information to the Request for Proposal (RFP) or to the announcement once you've received it. Then, you have the processes to determine how you are going to make things happen.

What activities and strategies will you implement? For instance, if you have ACT prep manuals, if you have the staff, if you have backpacks, what are you going to do with these things? If your mission is to better prepare students for college, and your goal is to increase ACT scores, how do you do this?

From there, you will see that your key performance indicators will determine your output and expedite your outcomes. What will be the results from giving backpacks or from including ACT prep manuals in the backpacks? A possible output could be the number of backpacks distributed or the number of students who now have ACT prep manuals. Even more important than output is outcome. Your outcome refers to what degree you have accomplished your goal(s). For example, if the goal is to improve math skills, your outcome might be that students who received a backpack and ACT prep manuals have improved their math scores.

The impact of all of this would be that those who receive the backpacks, manuals and participate in supportive service activities presented by your program have enrolled in college or have expressed interest in college enrollment (depending on your goals).

Impact changes one's environment, situation, or circumstance. In this example, attending college could potentially change a situation, circumstance, or environment. A mistake that is often made when asking for funding is that we look too closely at the output (the number of people we serve) before paying enough attention to the outcome (the results of services) and impact, the change or transformation that our service makes.

Not knowing how to address output versus outcomes, versus impact makes it more difficult to convince a funder that your organization does change lives or solves a problem.

Nevertheless, despite not knowing how to address programs, most organizations will argue that funding is their leading need and not program development. There is no argument. You certainly need money. You need clients. You need staff. You need material and resources. These are the things that the money will pay for. However, you also need relationships. You need partnerships. You need data. You need accountability. These are the things that move you more expeditiously into sustainability and success.

GRANT FACTS

Grants are great. Everyone wants them. Although grants are a joy to have, they can be not so fun to manage. It is important to remember that no matter who is writing the grant, no matter their previous or current grant approval rate, no grant is guaranteed. Many new and under-experienced organizations are led to believe that a nonprofit approval status or, in today's time, a business formation, in general, is all that is necessary to receive grant funding. This is far from the truth.

While a nonprofit determination, and in the case of for-profit grants, a documented business formation is required to get your foot in the door, these pieces of paper alone do not mean that you are competitive or even qualify for select grant funding opportunities. In the case of nonprofit and public charities, your determination letter will state to some degree that your organization is "eligible" for gifts (including grants). Nevertheless, eligibility is not the same as qualified or competitive. Again, everybody wants a grant because that's money that is free money, right? You don't have to pay it back. So, in terms of free, that's what that means.

Of course, depending on the grant that you are awarded, there are typically a couple of strings attached. There are reporting and management that must be done and compliance concerns. So... nothing is free after all. And they're not guaranteed. This is not the student financial aid or need-based application process. Organizations can't simply report need and receive funding.

Now, don't get me wrong, some grants, particularly mini-grants, and sponsorship-type awards, are a bit easier to obtain (although still not without competition and subjective selection processes). Take, for example, the Walmart Foundation Local Community Grants. They don't ask for a whole lot of information, but they typically award between a couple of hundred dollars and a couple of thousand dollars to various community-based organizations.

While mini grants are a great source of funding, most organizations look for larger grants and additional support when they are truly focusing on sustainability. Your organization is going to have to be in good shape to attract the funding that you desire to attract.

Knowing how and what to do and what not to do increases your chances of winning the grant. In addition to grant writing, I have spent a great amount of my time serving as a grant reviewer for grantmaking institutions, foundations, agencies, and corporations of all sizes. Many applications start out on the wrong foot, making it difficult to recover and successfully endure the grant review process.

Sometimes something as seemingly simple as your program or project name can be the start of a negative review. My favorite way to decide on a program name is to think about the desired program results and name the program to reflect the outcome.

For instance, if the intended outcome is to engage more community members in mathematics, the program might be named something like "Math Matters." Before jumping into any grant application or funding opportunity, it is important to know whether or not your organization is a good fit for the funder, and vice versa. This starts with carefully researching the funder to understand its philanthropic goals, its funding patterns, its core values, and application criteria. One major question to ask yourself is, "Are they wanting to fund what I wish to have funded?" Remember that these opportunities are less about you and more about whether or not your organization can meet the needs of the funder.

A well-written funding announcement, "Request for Proposal" (RFP) and "Notice of Funding Opportunity (NOFO), etc., will tell you exactly what it is they want to support, and what it is they don't want to support. It will tell you what they pay for and what they don't pay for.

Again, research the funder, learn about them, and read the funding announcement in its entirety. Research the background of the funder, whom they've funded in the past, and what kind of organizations they like to fund. How much do they like to give?

We've talked a little about programs in a previous chapter, remember, you must have your program description and logic model ready before you apply for the grant. These are the tasks that you complete before the application. Applying for the grant is not the time to figure out what the program includes or what the program should look like? Or what and how we evaluate the program.

Before you look at another grant opportunity, sit down and think about what programs your organization offers right now and create a logic model for your programs or at least a detailed program description. What are the processes of your program, and what kind of goals and objectives does this program have? What's your potential impact for the program? You want to know that before you get into the grant opportunity.

Why? Because when you see the announcement and the announcement says we're funding XYZ or the funder says, "Our goal is to do XYZ." When your program is intended to serve the same purpose, you know right away that you are a good fit. If you are not a good fit, you also know that you should not apply for funding. This saves you time as well as the funder's time in review.

Once you have decided to apply, follow the instructions. That sounds easy. It's easier said than done, right? Sometimes we get into the applications, and they'll do things such as limit characters or word count or ask us for additional documents and audited financials.

Eliminating the fluff and getting straight to your answer as it relates to the question presented helps you to honor word count.

Additionally, while there are sparingly some work-a-rounds as they relate to audited financials depending on the funder, it is best to submit exactly what is being asked of you, exactly how it is being asked of you. If you are missing a financial audit and your reason for missing this is that you cannot afford an audit, this is a good sign that you are not ready for the type of funding you are seeking. Well-positioned organizations understand the need to budget for necessities such as audited financials if they are indeed ready to pursue the type of funding that requires such information. The funder wants to know that you are a sustainable organization.

If you cannot pay for things that are important to them, like an audited financial, they're not going to trust that you know what to do with their funds. They're not going to trust that you know how to manage your funds, and not going to trust that you know how to prioritize, which will make them think you're not ready for their funding.

On the other hand, you could indeed be ready for funding made by funders not requiring an audit, but for those that do, you would not be a competitive applicant since your organization is unable to submit all required documents.

Now, if they don't require one, you're good. If you have a relationship and existing relationship with the funder, you can reach out in some instances to the grant manager, and they may fill you in on any possible work-a-rounds.

Additionally, when responding to a funding announcement, it is critically important that you understand the focus areas of the funder and are assured that your area(s) of focus are relevant. For instance, if the funder wants to fund community service projects, your program should focus on community service and not a different focus area.

When describing your program to the funder, even if they do not ask you to specify, you want to know if your program is evidence-based, evidence-influenced/informed, or if it is something that you are honestly just experimenting with. Knowing that your programs are evidence-based or influenced/informed by an existing body of proven evidence helps you to determine how the programs will be evaluated.

Evaluation helps you to determine whether your program does what it is designed to do. This helps to communicate outcomes and impact. Funders also want to believe, based on your grant applications and the work that you have done, that you are an expert in your area of work, and you fully comprehend the challenges of those you serve.

Take, for example, your organization serves youth. You are assumed to be an expert in issues and concerns related to youth. If you are proposing things that don't make sense for your population, using measurement tools for evaluation that are outdated in the youth development field, using language or vernacular that does not fit your audience, etc., it is going to be hard to convince a funder that you are credible or knowledgeable enough to be trusted with their funding.

A sure way to convince funders that you cannot be trusted with their funding is to make the request for funding or make the proposal more about you than you make it about them, what they need for you to accomplish, and the problem that you solve.

It is often that we enter grant proposals thinking it is about us and what we need or want, like, seeking out funding because you want a building. However, you are not clearly communicating why. Why is the building needed? What does the building have to do with the people you serve? How does the building solve the problem for the people that you serve?

The same goes for salaries. Although there are tons of funding opportunities that wish to help with salary support, the ultimate goal of funders is to solve or address the problem(s), those you serve are faced with. In other words, your salary is not the problem of the funder. Your salary is your problem.

Honestly, the funder does not care if you are paid. While they know that work requires pay at some point, assuming that you will rely completely on grant funding to pay salaries, especially when your organization does not otherwise manage or attract a steady level of funding, is an unrealistic assumption. Ultimately, funders do not care if you volunteer for the rest of your life. For this reason, it is the responsibility of your organization to develop and obtain unrestricted revenues to assist with salary support.

Having other options for necessities, such as a salary, also helps funders see your ability to attract funding. They see your ability to generate revenue outside of your "asks" to them. This helps to convince them that their investment in your organization is a good one. They trust that because you know how to generate revenue, their investment is not in vain.

Let's say that the grant or funding opportunity is for one year, or more. If the grant is your only source of funding, and you have no other grant funding or funding from other sources, what happens when the funding ends? Are you going to fire everybody on the project? Is the project going to end? If that's a yes, then the funder just wasted money because your project does not go past the limits of their gifts. Investments, which is what funding is, should make a lasting impact.

Sometimes we are certainly worth funding, just not worthy of the amount that we are asking for when it comes to funding requests. Don't be greedy. Ask for what it takes to facilitate the results. The funding announcement says that the funder is awarding up to $250,000. Often, under-experienced organizations go for the gusto.

Nevertheless, when the funder reviews the proposal, the project description and scope of work more closely resemble $25,000 than $250,000. The funder can look at your proposal and know they don't need $250,000, despite how fancy your budget appears to be. Don't submit greed-based applications. Your applications should reflect the scope of work that you will perform or are performing.

Understanding your potential funder ahead of time, knowing the answers to the questions you will find in grant applications, and knowing how to answer them, puts you on track for success.

As leaders of your organization, you should be able to answer the questions in a grant application using your internal knowledge and resources, even in the absence of a grant writer. While a good grant writer can craft answers in the manner most appealing to the funder, you should know the answers. If you're having problems answering most of the questions in the application without a grant writer, that means that you're probably not ready for that grant or opportunity.

Likewise, if your requested budget or the amount you are asking for, especially in a grant proposal, does not make sense when compared to your program, a funder will not see you as funding worthy. Your program/project description should be a direct indication of what your budget will represent.

You're asking for a whole bunch of salary support when the funder clearly states that they are not supporting salaries. You are asking for random items that do not align with the work you are doing, or you are completely asking for things that the funder has communicated that they do not fund.

Sometimes we mean well, but we put the cart before the horse and possibly ride ourselves out of winning the award. Often, we present questionable implementation strategies, particularly when the capacity that we claim to have does not match the capacity's evidence by proven work and fiscal responsibility.

So… you have two staff members. Also, you're going to serve 10,000 people within the course of a year, and right now, you've only served maybe 500 people. How are you going to make this happen? What drastic change, as it pertains to staffing, program development, financial/fiscal development, and systems development are you going to do to ensure that you take the sudden leap from serving 500 to serving 10,000? How are these changes manifested in your requests? How is your current work showing that you have the capacity to bridge from serving 500 to 10,000?

Remember that this is somebody else's money, and they don't have to give it to you. To improve your funding worthiness, it is important that you understand the basics of evaluation on both an organizational and programmatic level. Organizational evaluation could be as simple as board assessments, satisfaction surveys for staff and volunteers, financial reviews, and audits, measuring milestones resulting from strategic planning, etc.

Programmatic evaluation helps the organization, and the funders know that you are doing what you were developed to do. How do I know that this works? How are you going to communicate that to the funder? Do you follow a case management process? Do you collect qualitative or quantitative data for your programs? Do you use existing measures? Are you implementing pre or post-test designs? Are you following a self-report strategy?

Let's say that you are providing tutoring services to 100 students. How does the funder know if you provided the service? How do you know that your tutoring service makes a difference? Have your students' grades improved? What kind of measurements are you going to use to measure the improvements in grades? What makes your tutoring service different, or how does it stand apart from similar services? How do you know that your tutoring service is sustainable?

We often ask for financial support when we should be developing in other areas first. This is not to say that we do not need the funding; this is to say that funders can trust us more if we do some internal work before we begin to seek external support. We find ourselves asking for money to help us to carry out programs where we really need to focus on strengthening our internal organization and our ability to sustain and strengthen our leadership.

Our organizations tend to appear weak when we want to rely solely on grants. We find it hard to attract them consistently and we continue to desperately look for grant funding or ask for sponsorships and donations unsuccessfully, because we have not done the inside work.

The inside work, which includes developing business and strategic plans, funding plans, program logic models, and succession plans, give us the guidance necessary to develop and help us to map out the process and associate it with a timeline that best serves our capacity.

TWENTY TRUTHS

I have over twenty years of experience in "non-profiting," it is what I do. I often find myself taking to social media to offer unsolicited comments regarding the need for organizations to focus on becoming funding worthy. Many of these comments equate to tangible tips for nonprofit success, while others communicate my thoughts as I work to do my part in developing funding-worthy organizations out here in these "nonprofit streets."

This chapter is a collection of my favorite "truths." Some of it shows you that I do have a little sense of humor, unfortunately, some of it is not too true to be funny.

If your organization seriously struggled financially in previous years (generated $0 to very few dollars), I am almost 100% sure that you will fall into one or more of these categories. (Don't argue. If this is you, just make it a goal to do better):

TRUTH One

- You did not do the work. Or if you did the work, your work was inconsistent.

- You waited for grant dollars that you weren't ready for, and when they didn't come, you didn't focus on other ways to bring in funds.

- You asked all the wrong people for money/support, and when you asked the right people, you asked them the wrong way, at the wrong time, and for the wrong reason.

- You thought that grants were the only way to fund your work... so you spent more time chasing them than you did positioning for them.

- You were all over the place as it relates to your mission, so you didn't know how to implement in ways that facilitate impact.

- You were listening to folk who told you that you could get funding but who failed to inform you that positioning and being competitive were necessary to attract it.

- You thought that people would give you money "just because" you have a 501c3 status.

- You didn't consider that nonprofit work requires the same or even more development energy as for-profit work.

- You were trying to be an organization of 1 and did not know how to utilize your team and/or board.

- You don't truly understand how your organization makes a difference and are finding it hard to show others that what you do is necessary and worth funding.

TRUTH Two

Walking Dead, Daybreak, The 100, Z Nation, Book of Eli, The Rain, All of Us are Dead, Falling Skies, Containment, The Colony .... Do you watch apocalypse-type, survivor shows or movies? My favorite is *Criminal Minds* on Netflix. Anyway, have you noticed that even in the most chaotic, confusing, unbelievable, unimaginable situations, folks are on the run, folks looking for cures, folks enduring or recovering from massive war, a wild "new world order"- people, zombies, pets, aliens or whatever still have problems that need to be solved, causes and issues to be addressed in the middle of an alien invasion.

For example, a character is experiencing domestic violence. Children are becoming zombies over there in that high school (*All of Us are Dead*), and nobody is coming to see about them (there was obviously no after-school mentoring program!)

Non-zombies seeking food and shelter, folks still trying to educate the kids in the communities, the frantic search for books and Bibles — a whole zombie apocalypse and folks are battling substance abuse issues. People are being captured and possibly wrongfully imprisoned. Children being born and looking for a safe place to play, people needing to know a trade/skill of some sort. Diseased people are ostracized and stigmatized, folk getting sick and need access to care, and a ride to the next safe city, but they don't have transportation. Some are stressed and depressed because of what's going on around them, the currency is confusing and unequally distributed, and so on.

I say all this to ask a question, "What is your organization's mission?" Come alien invasion or zombie apocalypse, if your organization was truly formed to solve a necessary problem, if it was truly formed to help people, you still must figure out a way to do it because you're still needed.

TRUTH Three

Why are nonprofits (especially new and underfunded ones) always almost immediately asking about money and support and how to get those things but never asking how to strengthen internal and external communications — how to properly develop and position?

In my very informed and strong opinion, most of these organizations are misguided or misinformed from the start. There is an "attractive hype" around going straight for funding, and the fact that most want to shortcut communications and development (even when we learn that these things are not only important but necessary for sustainability), which confirms the fact that most operate out of desperation.

Desperation makes you feel as though you don't have time to "do it right" … it makes you want to "do it right now." Desperation makes you fall for the hype … because the hype seemingly offers a quick solution to your problem (which you think is funding … but it's really not, it's the development and communications).

Stop being desperate. Desperation stinks. Scammers and spammers smell desperation from a mile away. Being desperate for funding makes you an easy target for the okey-doke. Take the time to develop yourself and your business.

Stop listening to pop-up coaches and consultants who are telling you to start a business so you can get grant money to "live your best life." Grant money (other people's money) is not for YOU to live YOUR best life. It's for the OTHER people (the people you serve).

Can you "earn" a salary from the nonprofit you run? Yes. You can and you should, however the keyword is "earn." It's a job, not the lottery.

Managing the grant is a larger responsibility than getting the grant. Congratulations! You got the grant...now what? Regardless of whether your funder has reporting requirements, you still have an obligation to utilize the funds as purposed by the funder, and to accurately account for and document its use.

A grant is not going to save you if you don't know how to make money. Funders want to know that they will have a good return on their investment, (the grant is their investment). If you are struggling to find a few dollars to properly form your business, a couple of dollars to develop your business presence, you are going to struggle to maintain your business after the grant money is gone. Funders have "trust issues." If they can't trust your ability to get started, they are not going to trust your ability to sustain.

Development is a process, and because most people don't like "process," the organizations that are led by individuals who want to skip it are not going to sustain and will stay stagnant.

TRUTH Four

In my years of working with nonprofit organizations, there are a few things that stand out about those seeking grant writers and those applying for grants.

Lots of the newer organizations with no solid foundation, process a grant rejection or unsuccessful application as "being burned by a grant writer," blame themselves for choosing what they feel to be a "bad writer," and sulk over the "loss" (that isn't really a loss because grants aren't guaranteed). Not surprisingly, these see more rejections than wins.

Organizations with more solid foundations usually see rejection as an opportunity to improve themselves internally. Will even ask the grant writer and/or funder (if permitted) what they can do better as an organization. Will understand that rejection is just a part of the process, and if they are confident that they are a solid foundation, they chalk the "loss" up to just understanding that "this one was not for them" or it simply wasn't their time, and they moved on. They also tend to win bigger and more consistently.

Unfortunately, many organizations fitting the #1 description are finding it harder to find good writers who want to work with them — this is because the characteristics of the organization in #1 scream "difficult client" and "desperation," and those two things don't work well together.

All obvious grant writing skills aside, as the leader of your organization, it is your responsibility to know the condition of your organization's foundation (whether you are ready for the type of grant you seek) before you attempt to hire a grant writer. If you are not "ready" for what you want... you need to be working on getting ready, you do not need to be working on a grant application.

TRUTH Five

When you make your "looking for a grant writer post" on social media.... also be sure to add things like:

- Whether your organization is an "actual" legal organization.

- Whether you have provided any "actual" services. Whether you have "actual" programs ... that you evaluate for "actual" outcomes.

- Whether you are producing "actual" impact and have proof of this.

- Whether you have a real functioning "actual" board. Whether you have an actual "budget." Whether what you are doing makes "actual" sense.

- Whether you understand your organization's "actual" readiness and competitiveness for the desired level of grant funding. Whether you understand what is required to manage an "actual" real grant.

- Whether you understand that grants are "actually" not guaranteed... no matter if they are written by the US Attorney General or the best writer, you can find on social media...

While a good writer is certainly worth more than his/her weight in gold...the proposal/grant application can only be as good as what YOU/The ORGANIZATION bring to the table. It is difficult to prove that you are ready to eat if you are not willing to contribute anything towards the meal, and by the way, that's the best way to starve!

TRUTH Six

Let's start budgeting for stuff that we need... Stop expecting that everything you "need" will be free (or dirt cheap). If you truly need it, budget to pay for it (even if it is offered somewhere for free). Budgeting for it gives you the understanding that funds need to be generated in order to obtain it... knowing that you need to generate funds helps you to adjust your mindset, do the work, and will better position your organization to attract what you need.

TRUTH Seven

You filed for tax-exempt status using the 1023EZ four months ago because you wanted to save money. Just four months ago, you told the IRS that you anticipate less than $50K in gross receipts, but as soon as you received your "Determination letter" in the mail, you posted on Facebook that you are "Looking for a grant writer" and you are seeking $100,000 in funding.

You are asking writers for their success rates and references, but you haven't successfully served anybody, don't have programs, people, or even a good plan... the better question is, "What is your success rate?"

TRUTH Eight

A. SCAM: I will get you a $100,000 grant. No documents or information is necessary. All organizations are eligible.

B. NOT A SCAM: I will write a grant for you up to the amount suggested by the funder ... but as represented by the proposed work and highlighted by your project description, evidenced by your demonstrated impact, supported by your mission-matched proof, record of service, and backed by your proof of fiscal responsibility.

A. SCAM: Jody took your money, shut down his Facebook page, and GONE.

B. NOT A SCAM: Bob asks you for documentation, questions your readiness, and asks questions about your organization before he agrees to write your grant.

The thing about "B" is that it requires work on your behalf. A LOT of folks DON'T want to do the work but want the reward.

TRUTH Nine

#1   There are those people who truly cannot afford it — I know because I've been one of those people.

#2   There are those people who can afford it but can't prioritize it, so they won't pay for it — I know because I've been one of those people.

#3   There are those people who can afford it but won't pay for it because you are giving it to them for free — I know because I've been one of those people.

#4 There are those people who understand the value of it, prioritize it, and find a way to afford it no matter what because they know they need it and don't expect it to be given to them — I know because I've been one of those people.

Those people in #2 and #3 are why ya'll are struggling with ya'll youth sports leagues/teams, etc. They are why you "think" you should be starting a nonprofit, (hoping that you get grants and other people's money) to help you pay for stuff that you think you need to give away for free because they are not prioritizing the need for it even when they can afford it.

Those people in #2 and #3 have individuals trying to start nonprofits so they can get a van donation to drop off their kids, but when you pull up to their house, there are four functioning cars in the yard, and licensed drivers on the couch watching Netflix.

Those people in #2 and #3 are posting on Facebook about how you are paying for stuff out of pocket. Asking how you can get a salary but scared to ask them to pay (and pay the right prices) for what you are providing.

As a people/community, we sometimes do more harm than good out of the intention of doing good. Some of us are training people to pass the responsibilities of what they need (or even what they want/depending on the situation) on others… making it impossible for them to prioritize the things that could take them and their children, in the case of your youth and sports programs to the next level.

Now the #1s are always there, and for this reason, we must act accordingly. But not everyone is a #1 — know what you're working with.

TRUTH Ten

The goal is not just to submit grant applications because there is a funding announcement. Some may be tired because you are consistently being denied funding. One reason for this is that you are looking for funding in all the wrong places.

The goal is to be/become a COMPETITIVE applicant!!

The "work and preparation" to become competitive starts BEFORE you enter the competition.

For example:

I honestly am in no shape at all to win an MMA fight, so I won't be signing up for any competition, not because I don't have faith but because I know that in the ring on fight day (or, in this case, the day you choose to respond to a funding announcement/submit a grant application) is not when I should be trying to get my stuff together.

Now, I could probably enter a slow-walking competition or something (I've had a little practice with that) and could probably win or at least have a good chance. But that's kind of the limit as it relates to my athletic abilities, so I must compete on my level, until I do what needs to be done to level up.

TRUTH Eleven

Stop mailing out all of these sponsorship letters to:

1) Folks who don't know you

2) Folks you don't know

3) Folks who don't care about / or don't know about what you do

4) Folks who have never heard of you

5) Folks you haven't established a relationship with

6)   Folks who don't like you or your organization

7)   Folks who are not connected to your cause

8)   Folks you have not researched

9)   Folks who don't have time to read your letter

10)   Folks you randomly select because somebody told you that "sending a sponsorship letter" is the best way to get sponsorships.

Ya'll are misplacing a lot of time and energy out here. Folk out here throwing ya'll's sponsorship letters in the trash.

TRUTH Twelve

And don't be out here asking folk to help you secure $250,000 in funding when you got a $25 fund development budget.

TRUTH Thirteen

You do not need a grant to fund your chicken sandwich restaurant business. However, you do need to sell chicken sandwiches.

TRUTH Fourteen

Reason #474647 why you're not being funded:

You are trying to sell your vision (what you hope to do "at some point in the future") to individuals who have yet to believe that you can walk out of your mission (what you are supposed to be doing "now").

TRUTH Fifteen

There is a difference between "storytelling" and "telling stories" (telling lies). Be careful about what you are putting in your grant applications just to get the money. Somebody might come back to look at that again... make sure that you are accurately representing your organization.

TRUTH Sixteen

If you are having a hard time finding the $500-$2000 (low-end) to complete and file your formation documents you're going to have an even harder time convincing a donor/funder/sponsor that you can generate the revenue needed to operate a sustainable business/organization — no one wants to give THEIR money to something that they don't believe can survive.

If their first encounter with you is focusing on your inability to obtain the things that are even required to make you "legit," AND you don't have a plan to convince them that you know what you're going to do to generate revenue, they are likely going to run in the other direction.

Folk are not just out here giving away THEIR money, "just because" YOU decided that you wanted a business/organization and you assumed that THEY would be your funding plan.

TRUTH Seventeen

I'm sorry to tell you, but there is no "Funding Fairy," there is no "implementation-free checklist, boot camp, workshop, workbook, grant writing class, screenplay... mini-series, made-for-TV movie, reality show (you get the picture) ... that will bring you other people's money if you are not putting in the work necessary to properly position, execute, and sustain.

How are you demonstrating that your organization is not only ready but worthy of the level of funding desired?

TRUTH Eighteen

You've been "self-funding" YOUR nonprofit public charity all these years because you keep thinking and acting like it's YOURS — this does not belong to YOU. Nonprofits, particularly public charities, are "by the people, for the people." But if you are going to insist on it being YOURS, WE (the people) are going to insist that you pay for it by YOURSELF.

TRUTH Nineteen

Being a "public charity" does not make you (the leader/the founder/the ED) a "charity case." Yes. You were formed to address a "charitable cause," but YOU are not a "charity case." Take the time to learn about the "business" of nonprofits. Businesses develop according to a process. If you are not in it for the process — now is a good time to get out of it. There are no overnight successes.

Invest (time and/or money) in what you need in order to develop and sustain your organization (this is what also compels others to invest in your cause). No one wants to give to folks who are not even giving to themselves UNLESS they are a charity case. You are not a charity case. You are a business — start acting like one.

TRUTH Twenty

One main reason why your organization is struggling is that: You can't write grants, you can't afford a grant writer, you think you must wait on the grant before you can do the work.... and you THINK that grants are the only way to fund it.

SUSTAINABILITY AND SUCCESS

Nonprofit sustainability refers to the ability of a nonprofit organization to continue its operations and achieve its mission over the long term without relying solely on external funding or donations. This includes, developing a diversified funding base, creating a strong organizational structure, building a reputation for effective programs and services, and creating a culture of efficiency and effectiveness. Additionally, nonprofit sustainability involves creating a long-term strategic plan, building a strong board of directors, and developing a culture of accountability and transparency.

At the end of the day, the funders want to see that your organization can stand the test of time. They want to know that you can walk out of your mission with or without their support. Funders do not wish to be your lifeline. In fact, it is too much of a burden on them to assume complete responsibility for your organization. Your ability to understand trends and changes as they relate to those you serve and the ability to maneuver through those changes shows the strength of your organization.

In addition to this, funding-worthy organizations know that the organization does not stop with the current leadership. Again, funders want to trust that your organization can stand the test of time. If there is a need to support your service population, the need will continue. With this, your service should also continue in one form or another despite who is in the leadership position. Nonprofit planning should involve a healthy look at succession.

Nonprofit succession refers to the process of planning for and implementing leadership changes within a nonprofit organization. This can include, identifying potential leaders and preparing them for leadership roles, creating a plan for transitioning leadership, and ensuring the continuity of the organization's mission and programs during the transition. It is an important aspect of nonprofit management and helps to ensure the long-term sustainability of the organization.

CONCLUSION

It is important for nonprofit organizations to not only serve a deserving population but also to have a clear and effective mission, strategic plan, and measurable impact. Funders and donors want to see that their resources are being used efficiently and effectively to make a real difference in the lives of the population being served.

Additionally, transparency and accountability are key factors in building trust with funders and donors. Nonprofit organizations should have clear financial reporting and governance practices in place and be willing to share information about their programs and outcomes.

Overall, while serving a deserving population is important, it is not the only factor in determining whether an organization is worthy of funding and support. Organizations must also demonstrate their effectiveness, efficiency, and transparency to gain the support of funders and donors.

ACKNOWLEDGEMENTS

Thank you to Shae Bynes for your "Kingdom Driven" nudges to complete this book.

Thank you to Ms. Carolyn White-Washington, Karen Glenn, Lorie Chinn, Tiffany Taylor-Hicks, and April Brooks-Dudley for your encouragement.

Thank you to my mom, Ms. Mae P. Gaffney for your love and support throughout the years.

Special thanks to my husband, Alexander, daughter, Alex'ah and two sons, Alec and Alex III, for holding me accountable and making this book a reality.

EXERCISES

While not exhaustive of the process, this chapter gives you an opportunity to assess your organization and your program(s). Understanding your mission and how to approach programs are important in positioning your organization to attract the necessary support. Independent of the need to build a strong foundation, inclusive of a solid and consistent board and team, being able to truly understand your mission and how it works to advance your organization increases your funding worthiness.

EXERCISE 1: A FUNDING WORTHY MISSION

What is your mission?

Good mission statements should be *clear, concise, and useful*.

Answer the following questions in one sentence each.

1.   Who do you serve?

2.   How do you serve them?

3.   What difference (or impact) does your organization make?

Now, placing the difference (impact) in front; write a clear concise and useful mission statement below:

Examples:

1.   Homeless individuals in Bullock County.

2.   Provide social support service and linkage to care.

3.   Improve their quality of life and overall well-being.

Mission - We improve the quality of life and overall well-being of homeless individuals in Bullock County, by providing social support and linkage to care services.

Answer the following questions about your organization:

1. Who are you?

    A. We know that you are a nonprofit, BUT what makes you, YOU? What is it at the core of your organization that makes you WORTH funding? How are you different from other organizations with similar missions? What impact would you like for your organization to be known for? How do you make a difference?

2. Who are you serving?

    A. What population are your services and programs created for?

    B. Do you serve a specific age group/ethnicity/demographic? If yes, discuss.

    C. Does your evidence support that this is who you are serving?

3. Statistically, how many have you served within the most recent 12 months?

4. Have you researched funding trends for your population? Does "the who you serve match who they want to give to?"

    A. How do you serve them?

    B. What are you doing?

    C.   What are the services that you provide?

          1.   What activities are your facilitating?

          2.   What are you allowing them to achieve?

5. What are you proposing to do based on your very next level of best (based on your mission and NOT on your vision)? Do you have the capacity to do this given the funds, skill, and staff that you are currently working with?

6. If you are provided with funding, how can you do more of what you are proposing?

7. Now that we know that you are serving, does this service make an actual difference? If yes, what is the difference? How are you measuring this difference (surveys, questionnaires, tests, observations, case studies)?

8. What are the 1-yrgoals and objectives of your activities and program? (List them for each of the services and activities you identified above).

How are you recording and reporting this? Are you using databases to track your progress? Which participant focused database are you using?

TIP: Understand the funder's area of interest/ Their area of interest should mirror your program/service goal.

EXERCISE 2: FUNDING WORTHY GOALS AND OBJECTIVES

Goals are measurable. Goals are short-term action steps that help you to meet your objectives. Goals are the process(es) that facilitate your objectives. Objectives are the end.

For example:

Goal: To teach 3 classes on positive self-thought by July 3.

Objective: To increase positive self-thought among course participants.

List 3 goals for your program and 3 objectives.

Identify 1 service area /program focus (the focus of your funding application or ask). What you provide here should be FOCUSED enough that your funder knows that you are committed to a direct area of service or collection of "related" services.

GOALS	OBJECTIVES

EXERCISE 3: BE WORTH SPONSORING

1. I identify at least 3 potential sponsors or corporate sponsors (relevant to your mission and as determined by your mission match to their philanthropic goals, core values, and funding practices).

1	
2	
3	

Note: For the purpose (s) of this assignment, your **target audience** includes those from whom you are requesting funding and support. Your **priority population** includes those you serve.

2. Describe your target audience. Describe funders identified above. For each one, discuss:

   A. What is their size and reach (for example, local, state, national, international)

   B. Are they committed to supporting your priority population? If yes, how so?

3. For each of the 3 potential funders, describe how forming a relationship with them, or being connected with them for support, benefits your organization. What's in it for your organization?

   For example:

   A. Increased exposure

   B. New support

   C. Improved credibility

   D. Associates your brand with the values of the sponsor (philanthropic goals)

What do the above examples (of others you have considered) look like for your organization?

4. What's in it for them (tell them how they benefit)?

   For example:

   A. Improved community perception

   B. Exposure to new clientele

   C. Higher consumer support

   D. Opportunity to win customers from competing

   E. Increased employee satisfaction and morale

What do the above examples (of others you have considered) look like for your organization?

5. For each of the 3 potential funders, are you seeking them for monetary contribution (gift or grant), in-kind contribution or support, or monetary sponsorship?

FUNDER	TYPE OF SUPPORT

What makes you unique (as it relates to how you serve, who you serve, and what impact you make) when compared to other organizations like yours?

- How do your programs differ from other organizations in the industry and in your area?
- Do you approach services and programs differently than others? If yes, how?
- What would happen if your organization did not exist?

EXERCISE 4: A WORTHY PROGRAM

Processes	Outputs	Input
What do you need in order to make this work?	How are you going to make this work? What activities?	What happened as a result of the activities?

Outcomes	Impact	Budget & Evaluation
What changes did the outputs produce?	How do the outcomes benefit your community and your population?	How much does it all cost? What tools and measures will be used to confirm that it works?

Consider a program or event. Depending on your goals, all outcomes below may not be achieved.

Anticipated Outcomes for Program Participants

What outcomes do participants need to achieve in order to have their needs met? Consider:

Changed knowledge (short-term outcomes)?

Changed behaviors (intermediate outcomes)?

Changed attitudes, values, conditions, status, etc. (long-term outcomes)?

Anticipated Outcomes for Program Participants (Cont.)

If you have identified several outcomes, then consider which are the most important outcomes to achieve and in what order?

From those most important outcomes, attempt to identify short-term, intermediate, and long-term outcomes.

Short-Term Outcomes (three to six months after program)

Intermediate Outcomes (six to 12 months after program)

Long-Term Outcomes (12-24 months after program)

Are there any remaining activities that you believe should be carried out to identify the most relevant, realistic, and important outcomes to pursue?

When responding to a funding announcement, take into consideration what the funder is wishing to fund.

What is the scope of what you are doing?

    I. How many participants/clients are in your program or proposed program or how many do you propose serving at your event (if your ask is event specific)?

        A. How much funding does it take to facilitate the program (or host your event)?

        B. What staff/support do you need?

        C. What other supplies, equipment do you need?

        D. How did you arrive at this scope (Have you conducted research? Is this based in evidence or experience? (Discuss)?

        E. Does this scope make sense as it relates to the size of the problem in your community? Discuss.

II. How much are they willing to give (what's the award amount) for each potential supporter (if you have reviewed possible opportunities)?

III. How much are they willing to give (what's the award amount) for each potential supporter (if you have reviewed possible opportunities)?

A. How much should you ask for (see scope).

B. Have you received this level of funding in the past?

C. If you were the funder, would you trust YOUR ORGANIZATION with the amount of funding you are requesting?

- Do you have a track record for managing funds? Explain.

- Have you shown the ability to produce results with the services you provide? Explain.

- Have you communicated that YOUR ORGANIZATION needs funding (is there a need for your organization, do you have a waiting list, are you serving at a desired capacity, is there evidence that your community desires more of what you have)? Discuss.

Making sense:

>Does it make sense? Your proposal tells a STORY... items in your budget should correlated with the direction of your proposal. For every action or process in your proposal (the content program description portion of your application) a budget item or items should be reflected by this action. For example, if your program describes a case manager, there should be an item for case manager in your budget.

Note: When asking for salary support

a. Is your staff qualified for the position that you are seeking payment for? Does their resume prove it? Will you have to hire?

b. Does the amount of work needed on the project reflect the amount of funds you are asking for in support of this work?

SUSTAINABILITY CHECKLIST

The ability to sustain your programs and organization go far beyond grants. This checklist includes ways to financially sustain your organization. Understand how your organization is positioned using this checklist will assist you tremendously when communicating your plan for sustainability to funders/potential funders.

Based on your organization's current strengths. How feasible is it to implement to strategies listed below (indicate by placing an X in the column for "very feasible" and "not at all feasible".

Strategy	Very Feasible	Not At All Feasible	Explain
1. Sharing positions and resources			
2. Becoming a line item in an existing budget			
3. Incorporating activities in organizations with similar missions			
4. Applying for grants			
5. Tapping into personnel resources			
6. Soliciting in-kind support			
7. Implementing fundraisers			
8. Pursuing third-party funding			
9. Developing a fee-for-service structure			
10. Acquiring public funding			
11. Securing endowments and planned giving arrangements.			
12. Establishing membership fees			
13. Strengthening and utilizing community partnerships			

Printed in the USA
CPSIA information can be obtained
at www.ICGtesting.com
LVHW061746030224
770460LV00126B/342/J